Wonderful

By Tanya Crowley

Do you know my Father in Heaven?
I call Him Papa.

He made EVERYTHING,
and He can do ANYTHING!

I can tell He is **WONDERFUL** because everything I learn about Him makes me say ...

I planted a seed in the garden.
I watered it and watered it and *WATERED* it.

But it didn't grow!
I couldn't make it grow.

But my Papa made it grow for me!

Papa is wonderful. He helped my seed burst up toward the sun.

Have you ever seen a real frog?

I used my GREEN crayon to draw a picture of one.

But my Papa made the real one,
and it was wonderful.

I couldn't stop
watching it until
it hopped away.

When I looked out the window, it was still too cold, and I didn't want to freeze into an ice block.

I thought I'd be stuck inside forever!

But while I was learning to wait patiently inside, my Papa had been moving the dark clouds away.

...so I could play in the wonderful warm sun.

My Papa is WAY bigger than the *WHOLE WORLD!*

I once thought He wouldn't be able to find me when I called for Him.

But my Papa already had a wonderful plan for that.

Even though He's so BIG, He makes sure He ALWAYS stays close enough to hear everything I say.

Yesterday the grown ups were sooo boring.
I said "I'll never, ever find something fun to do
if I have to just sit here".

But my Papa is so wonderful.
He made sure there was someone there just for me!

I didn't want to leave until Grandpa finished telling me all about his ancient telephone.

Mum said it doesn't rain in the outback much like it did here last night. That means there isn't much water to drink.

I need a big glass of water when I'm thirsty or I'll die!

I wonder how everything stays alive in the outback if there's hardly any water?

My wonderful Papa must give them a drink!

Collecting the eggs used to be my most favourite thing to do each morning.

But not anymore!

My Papa gave us a wonderful surprise this morning.

Papa made the world so big and full of so many wonderful things!

But guess what!?!

He made a world just as wonderful and big under the sea!

"What is it?!" said Grandpa

"What is it?!" said Uncle Justin

"What is it?!" said Nanna

"What is it?!" said the neighbour

"What is it?!" said Leila

But I was way too excited to stop and talk.

I just had to get outside as soon as I heard the icecream truck.

Do you think icecream is Papa's most wonderful idea too?

The Wildlife Sanctuary was so much fun!
I can't wait to visit again and see all the animals.

I think maybe my Papa thinks some of them are a little bit funny looking.

But I think they are all WONDERFUL!

My neighbour loves flowers *sooooo* much.

She keeps telling me about ALL of them ALL the time!

I don't think I'll ever remember anything she told me.

But that's OK.
She said not everyone loves the same things.

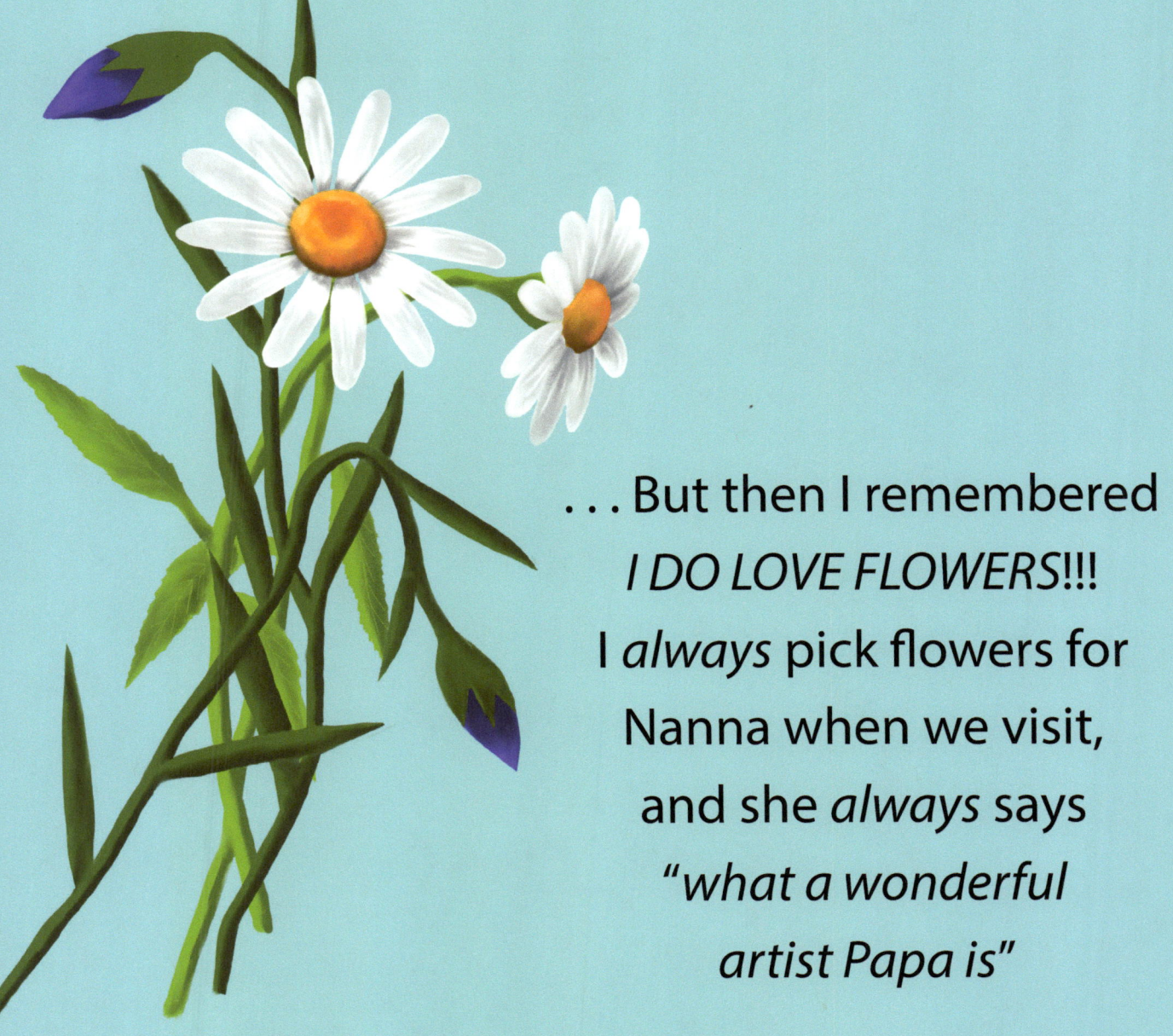

. . . But then I remembered
I DO LOVE FLOWERS!!!
I *always* pick flowers for
Nanna when we visit,
and she *always* says
*"what a wonderful
artist Papa is"*

On the way to our holiday I was really grumpy.

I was so annoyed I even said out loud,
"How can anyone sit for this long in a car!"

But not long after, I remembered Papa always gives me wonderful ideas when I'm bored.

My sister even thought it was a fun idea!

I was telling my friends all about how WONDERFUL my Papa is . . .

. . . and how WONDERFUL He has made so many things.

We even thought we could make a book about it!

... But I said "There's too many WONDERFUL things about Papa to fit in one book!"

Published in Australia
by Tanya Crowley

© Text, Digital Illustrations and Cover Design
Tanya Crowley, 2025
tcrowleybooks@gmail.com

Cataloguing-in-Publication data is available from
the National Library of Australia.

ISBN 978-0-6454836-5-9

www.ingramcontent.com/pod-product-compliance
Lightning Source LLC
Chambersburg PA
CBHW041203290426
44109CB00003B/118